In Search of Bliss

By J.L. Rainey

For Zuzu

Who gave me a life of dreams, passion and love…

For information, write to:
Strategic Alliances Publishing
P.O. Box 470967, Brooklyn, NY 11247

Design and layout by:
Sheri Collins for Shadez Communications.

J.L. Rainey

In Search of Bliss

ISBN 978-0-9798052-0-2

Dedicated to every being…

In Search of Bliss

ACKNOWLEDGMENTS

This book unfolded like life itself … flowing mysteriously and effortlessly.

There are so many people whose love and support I'd like to acknowledge on my own personal journey toward bliss. Instead of individual thanks, I give thanks to each and every person who has ever crossed my path, touched my life or been in my presence. Each of you has helped me to grow in my own divinity and purpose.

Each of you has been a powerful mirror for my dreams, goals and aspirations—my hope is that I have been equally as beautiful to you.

One Love, One Soul.

Namaste

TABLE OF CONTENTS

When I was eleven years old my mother gave me the most beautiful gold ring for my birthday. Even though she told me to only wear it on special occasions, I decided to wear it so I could show it off to all my friends.

I was so proud of the ring that I even let different friends try it on throughout the day.

When it was time to go upstairs, I realized that I had lost the ring. I searched for it as long as I could before I finally had to go upstairs and confess the loss to my mother.

I continued to search for that ring for days and weeks on end. Even today, the loss of that ring feels like a part of me—is missing.

Question:

Why do we search for peace, love, and joy?

Is it possible that we once had it and lost it?

Places, Spaces and Things

A LONGING FOR HOME

Tears run down the face of an innocent child
Raining down and drenching her
As when a poorly forecasted storm
Rages against the shoreline—breaking barriers
       Not yet built
For lack of time and preparation.
Tears run down
       Because shame is being placed in her temple
        At her alter of purity
Now being defiled by the elder priest and scribes
Who created and molded a system where the exterior
       Is exalted,
But there is a failure to see the spirit of life within.
Tears for herself and them
Because she knows she has been initiated into their
  Ways—into their being afraid,
Alone, and of Sin.
She will no longer pass by a caterpillar in pure
       Excitement—of what is to come.
She will be like them—
       Only seeing what is not.
Only seeing
That she has come too early
Or regretting that she has arrived too late.
Tears run
Because she cannot run
Fast enough   *back,*   *back*
To the place
       Where she was   *free.*

I cannot seek anything;

I can only be the thing

I seek.

All experience—is only as real

As I make it.

The law of life says

That matter is neither created

Nor destroyed.

I am a part of the cycle of matter.

therefore

I am neither created nor destroyed.

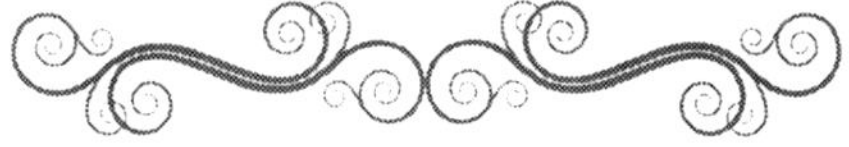

My life began the moment that

I admitted my inability to control everything—or
anything

COMING UNDONE

Two lives intertwined by experience,
Now juxtaposed
In contrast
Rather than integration.
There is no prose, line, or rhetoric that can ease the tension.
Each word spoken
Illuminates the pretense
Of the other (life).
Sacred whispers are uttered
In the hope
That truth will enter spaces, yet touched.
Two lives
Coming undone.
Here, one will blossom
With fruits ripened and nourished
By healing light.
The other
Gasps for last lingering breaths
Of   powerless   utterances,
Strangled
By cords of inquiry
And insight.
Each thought spoken
        silently
Illuminates the deceit
Of   One   false   self.
Two lives, each one mine,
Transcending the boundaries   self imposed.

Coming together
In this moment to recreate life itself.
Each word creates life.
Each word, spinning worlds off axis,
Causing planets to align in harmony
With my word.
          With my word
Worlds are born,   and life appears
As a majestic inspiration of this truth.
I,
Here,
Now,
Am present to the two lives
As
A reflection
Of all lives.
Coming forth
To reveal the sacred truth
Once uttered
Beyond
This space and time—that
I,
We,
All,
Are everything
Juxtaposed
In contrast
To   Nothing.

Only when I admitted the frailty of my humanness

did I find the courage and strength

to turn within

and find the eternal beauty of my soul.

It is impossible to clean up my mind

Before I clean out my home.

If I don't—the clutter of both will return as soon as I
turn my back.

The only place I can be

Is where I am.

What I resist—Persists.

I AM

I reside in constellations
As boundless as Pleiades,
joining in union with Polaris.
I am
Love in its purest form.
I exist in eternity,
Light years away.
If you seek me,
I will reach you
just in time
For you to comprehend
That as my form is of light,
That which you see
Has already transformed.
Your fixation
And
Admiration
of that which you see
Is only a perception
of that which you
Wish   to   see,
Because you find comfort
In the limitation of your definitions
that hold and encase me.
If in this moment
you were present

To see me as I truly am,
You would already know
That I,
As You,
Are light,
Being born of light,
Escaped from form,
Free and Boundless
As the nights sky.
See the reality of me,
And you will be free.

Work on your own life before you

begin working

on someone else's.

People treat you

as you treat yourself.

I am all that exists

There is *no* Thing that I am *not*

Therefore everything that exists

Is part of who I am.

RAIN: A MEDITATION

Circling within a formation of rainbow colored sky
I watch you closely
Listening for my music of angelic voices
A choir of thunderous roars
whose melody is a multitude of children laughing
May I visit you today?
I raise my eyes
through clouded streams of blue cotton candy
whose twirling marshmallows create windswept horizons
My time is coming
I will beckon my children into an arch
to strike an arrow of white hot fire
Icy heroines will burn these clear blue cotton marshes
Leaving only indigo embers
from west sky to east sky
Will you dance with me now?
The tide has pushed back the unassuming shore
Mountains have gently echoed into the belly of the forest
that awaits me
Every life
Whether it moves, has moved or will move
Seeks my nectar
Will you sit and dine with me?
My table is a scepter of wine
Spread within earth, wind, fire and air
Who dare deny this invitation?
I am your joy

Can you feel my intent in the eyes of children playing with
sand?
Can you know my love?
As it stands over you
in the shade of summer's day
I am that tallest tree
Every blade of grass which houses the smallest of these/ them
Every drop of ocean water
Salted
As each tear you cry
I am you
Can you see me?
I/ mirror/ soul
Indeed you drink of me
As I drink of you
When you return to our mother
Will you call my name?
And not say
come back another day
Drink of my blessing
Know that I am here
for you
For I am here!

नमस्ते

NAMASTE

It was there
transcending space and time,
Invading each breath,
Reaching forward
to touch.
Beating heart—
Seeking truth,
Facing the divine,
Soothing the longing
in my soul.
Crying unto God,
Reflected in touch,
You—
The oneness and union
made real.

Relationships

Joy is watching a newborn baby in all of its innocence.

Generosity is interacting with adults as if they were as innocent as children.

Everyone who enters my life

For more than five minutes

Has an important lesson to teach me;

If for less than five minutes—I have a lesson to teach them.

My daily prayer:

That you see the very best in you,

when you look into my eyes.

That you hear the very best about you,

when I open up my mouth.

That you know the very best of you,

in the way that I treat you

This is the mirror I wish to be.

Even a murderer is worthy of Namaste.

Which is more dangerous?

Loving another human being more than I love God?

Believing that love for another human being can ease
my pain?

Believing I love God more than God loves me?

Serving God out of fear and obligation?

None of these is dangerous;

Each leads to discovering my truest Self.

LOVE ACTUALLY

There is no doubt
that I am being consumed.

I watch myself,
watch myself,
watching you.

I memorize and celebrate the essence of you.

I could,
if I were a painter, create a canvas
that would surely come to life as a silhouette in tribute to your
inner beauty,

I would sculpt your likeness by heart.
Even Michelangelo
would bless you
as perfection.

In my heart's mind
I always know
And remember
The arch of your neck,
The curve,   and the bend
That gracefully summons images of grazing gazelles.

That swooping curl
        that caresses and dances upon your face
        beckons a gentle kiss.

None could deny that this is sensuality itself.

I have remembered
In eternity
That sleeping breath that seduced my soul last night,
Sounding like gentle waterfalls and roaring oceans—
Simultaneously.

Your hands,
Perfectly suited to craft poetry,
                                        Novels, paintings,
            And art
or any and all things sacred
Seems in my mind a perfect match
To hold mine —Me —us —gently.

The laughter that echoes from your belly
Heals every hurt in me   as it dances
                    Around my heart.

Without any effort on your part
You are showing me
        places where love yearns to be.

Your gaze
Is warm—   like fresh-baked bread,

Urging every part of my being
To be touched and inspired.
Patiently
Waiting
For the cooling—so that I may savor the serving.
Warm, buttery, and delicious,
One serving
Is never enough.

So,
I memorize,
I remember,
I watch,
In order that I may nourish myself of you
For the times
That   I   am   without you,
Because my love for you
Must be memorized by heart.

The most powerful person in the world

is the person who helps another person

become more powerful.

When the world believes that love

no longer exists,

Can I be the one

to remind them—

That I am still here ?

Even the most competitive person will stop competing

when I offer them my heartfelt assistance.

Love never injures. It is not in its nature.

If I have ever been injured, it is impossible that it was done by an act of love.

PARADOX

The silence
within the abyss
Replacing what was once familiar
Stirring the echoes of past betrayals
The truth unspoken

The divide could be no wider.

Love of self
inconceivably, reconcilable with self love
Stepping across the divide
Seemed meaningless
However,
longed for
like breath, air, truth
I am suffering for love
Suffering for the truth or shades thereof
Clinging to the familiar emptiness
Yet grasping for the time when love was

Creating voids
moving toward you
yet away
My mind traveled to past illusions
This time
The words shattering the pretense of safe exchanges
I am empty
Not of myself

But of the energy
which once filled my being
In the form of your touch, your gaze
Filling sacred spaces which cry out to be recognized

My soul shouting, "Hear me. Feel Me. Hold Me"
Transcend the fear of yesterday
And embrace the wholeness of your BEING

The thoughts of my thoughts are "Where is the heart of you?"
Has it sought the arms of another?
Why?
Is it because you are whole now?
Or
Is your love contained in the boundaries of self preservation?

Redirected?
As a river which has known too many days of drought?
Seeking new outlets which nourish and replenish the source?

I am crossing these channels
This unfamiliar territory
Wading carefully
Afraid, as the tide rises
Bringing in waves
That pull me off my center
As the waters
Crush my bones.

The silence of the water
Bathe me
Yet dreams recreate the experience, drowning me
Shattering my thoughts
Fears shout at me from hidden corners of
Consciousness
Clinging to mind-made fantasies
Beckoning me to journey into this abyss
Which knows no love....
Which can know no joy.....
Which covers sacred spaces in order to choke out
The breath of being whole.
Fear
Clinging to suffering
Always moving toward shades of self betrayal
For it is there that soul re-emerges
Transcending boundaries of self preservation
Seeking the silence
Within
The abyss
Where I rise as my Self
In all my majestic glory
Hear me. Feel me. Hold me
And embrace the wholeness of my being
Both
Flesh and Soul
Having embraced the void
Shattered the pretense of safety
Crossed the abyss

In order to grow, one must face the unknown.

Therefore—is the result of fear the inability to grow?

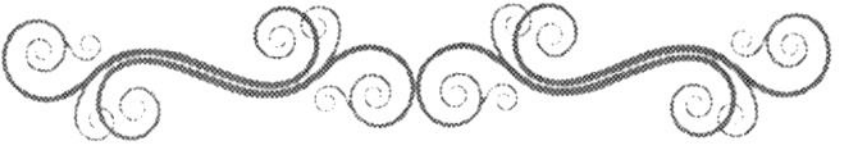

Arrogance and low self-esteem are equally damaging.

No one likes to be in the presence of either. One is bitter, the other boring.

Neither is honest.

If Moses aged 40 years when looking upon the face
of God for one second—

Is it really possible that the fullness of God

could exist within one human being

without turning them into ash?

If I truly believe in a Supreme Being—God,

Would I or could I ever be lonely—or alone?

Which life would you choose?

Having one dollar with eternal peace, or having a net worth of a billion dollars, without ever experiencing joy?

Which life would I choose? I would choose a life of peace with the one dollar. Perfect peace always creates a path to abundance.

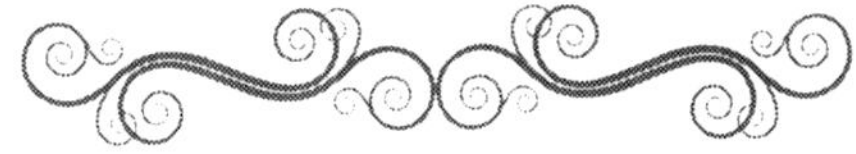

Even children playing in a sandbox

Know

To give as good as they get.

As much as I appreciate modern education, I've often wondered how come

No one has ever taught me how to achieve

Serenity.

If we were honest, we would admit to ourselves that we don't actually believe that we were made in God's image.

We are much more comfortable making God—in our own image.

I like the idea of reincarnation:

It limits my ability to stereotype, label, or put people into boxes.

Reincarnation, if true, means I've been a man, white, Jewish, Asian, Indian, gay, straight (and so on, and so on)—more than a few times.

Truth is sweeter than honey.

Wisdom is brighter than sunlight.

However, neither is as powerful as a being,

Who chooses to live consciously.

The day is coming

When kings will serve, rulers will uplift,

And leaders will be role models of peace.

I create this reality for myself in each and every moment.

If you knew that God was looking for you

Even more urgently than you've been looking for
God,

Wouldn't that make you feel better than you've felt
in a really long time?

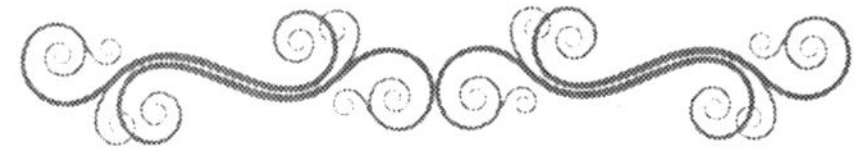

If I trust myself—I will trust you.

If I see myself—I will see you.

If I love myself—I will love you.

These are inescapable laws.

Passion—is like dominoes.

Once it starts flowing over,

There's an effect

Of miracles everywhere you turn.

If life were a movie

I'd rather be the director than an extra!

If merely thinking positively

could make life work.

Slavery, War, Murder, Racism and Poverty,

would never have come into existence.

Act forever young;

Be forever eternal.

The biggest mountains reside in your mind.

Perception is the ability to inform your vision of
what the truth is,

As opposed to your vision informing you

of what the truth might be.

No one is ever angry to the point

That a smile and a little bit of cooperation—

Won't melt their heart

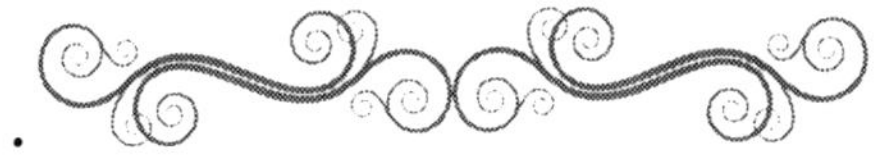

Children become what they see, hear, feel, and
experience.

Are you any different?

I'm starting a diet—

I'm reducing my intake of negativity;

Adding an ounce of sweetness to my conversations;

Drinking eight more glasses of compassion;

Racing the treadmill of tolerance;

Practicing a mile of gratitude,

even before I start my day.

Who knows—

By next year I might be ready to run a

Wisdom marathon.

If I substitute the word "challenge"

For "opportunity"

life becomes a stepping stone

Instead of feeling like a mountain

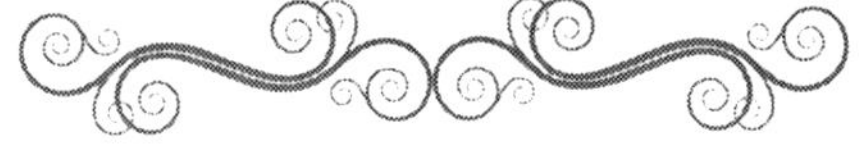

When a rainy day is a mess,

And a sunny day is unbearable,

The eye of the beholder

Has created them both.

Smile as often as you think;

Love as often as you breathe;

Serve as often as you blink.

Then—Do it again.

Beliefs and ideas are like clothes:

You should try them on

Before you wear them out in public;

Never wear the same ones everyday;

And if everyone's looking at you as if you're crazy—

It might be time for a makeover.

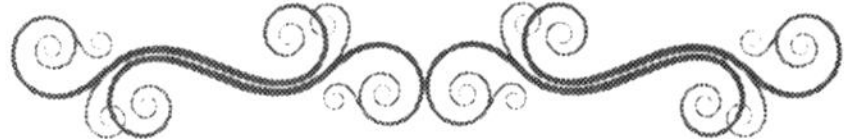

STRESS:

Soulfully desired

Transformation

Reduced to an

Emotionally

Stimulating

Substitute

The definition of the word sin is to miss the mark.

Without sin we cannot develop or expand our consciousness.

Consequently, a life without sin

Is a life without growth!

Affirmations are personal (like your toothbrush),

Based on your vision (hello, life experience),

And your goals (uh…can you say uniquely individual)?

So instead of claiming that affirmations don't work,

I say, try making up your own, before you—throw away someone else's toothbrush.

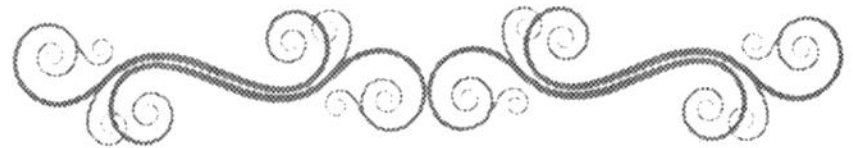

Steps to Achieving Wealth:

Step 1:

Believe it's Possible.

Step 2:

Visualize Your Path to Wealth.

Step 3:

Experience Your Wealth—Now

(view, visit, vibrate).

Step 4:

Perform the Necessary Actions.

Step 5:

Say Yes To Everything That Doesn't Hurt You.

Instead of beating myself up for not having enough
hours in the day to meditate—

I have decided to create my own methods of
meditation:

Dishing Dharma:
I visualize my dream vacation as I wash the dishes.

Mopping Mantra:
Repeat positive words while swinging that stick.

Karma Cooking:
I now view preparing dinner as an act of service.

Why don't you create a few of your own?

____

____

Your measure of success is not found in
dollars and cents.

Success is your ability to sense success irrespective of
the dollars and cents.

Before we are rich, we are visionaries.

Before we are bold, we are courageous.

Before we are powerful, we are self aware.

And once we possess all of the above:

Fear is incapable of governing our choices.

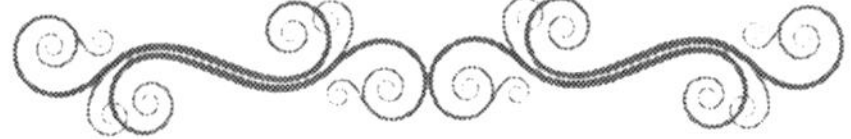

Share from a place of prosperity

And the Universe will open its gifts to you

Like flowers blossoming in the dawn of spring.

Sharing your heart

with an angry and bitter person,

Is like giving a stranger keys to your mansion.

It's guaranteed

That they will take—

more than they give.

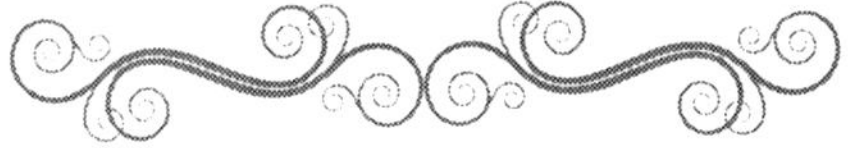

Give everything you have to life

And life will give everything it has to you.

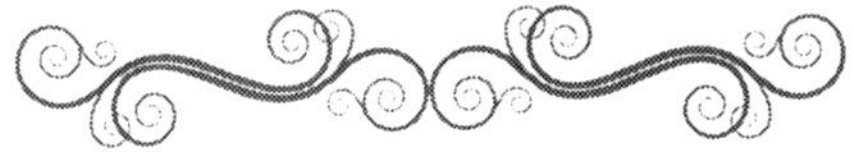

Create your own commandments.

What you feel and what you think is

different from what you know.

Gossip is a form of violence that has many victims.

1: The person being talked about;

2: The listeners;

3: The Universe—

And such a waste of words!

The sun rises and sets, then rises once again.

The tide moves from high to low, and rises once again.

The moon waxes and wanes from nothingness to fullness, then rises once again.

The seasons change from hot to cold, then cycle once again.

Could human life be any different?

I think not.

Today is the last time I use the word *death*.

Bliss is—

As you are.

Bliss Speaks—

As You Speak.

Bliss Seeks, As You Seek.

Because Bliss Remembers Who You Were Born To
Be,

Remember Bliss—and you will remember who you
are.

Birth

Is the moment when

We agree to forget

Everything we've already learned,

In order

To become better than we already were.

This is the journey to Bliss.

To be continued …

Namaste

Breinigsville, PA USA
28 August 2009
223134BV00001B/1/P